HENRY DAVID THOREAU
THE POET'S DELAY

HENRY DAVID THOREAU
THE POET'S DELAY

A Collection of Poetry by America's
Greatest Observer of Nature

Illustrated with Watercolors by
WINSLOW HOMER & JOHN SINGER SARGENT
and other Masterworks from the
MUSEUM OF FINE ARTS, BOSTON

RIZZOLI
NEW YORK

Published in 1992 by
MUSEUM OF FINE ARTS, BOSTON
Department of Retail Publications
295 Huntingon Avenue
Boston, Massachusetts 02115
and
RIZZOLI INTERNATIONAL PUBLICATIONS, INC.
300 Park Avenue South
New York, New York 10010

Endsheet photography of Walden Pond © Roland
Robbins, 1992, used by kind permission of Geraldine
Robbins. Frontispiece is Portrait of Thoreau by Samuel
Worcester Rowse © 1992 Concord Public Library, and is
reproduced by kind permission.

Library of Congress Cataloging-in-Publication Data

Thoreau, Henry David, 1817-1862
    Henry David Thoreau—the poet's delay : a collection
of poetry /
by America's greatest observer of nature ; illustrated
with watercolors by Winslow Homer & John Singer
Sargent, and other masterworks from the Museum of
Fine Arts, Boston ; compiled and edited by Kathryn
Sky-Peck
               p.   cm.
    1. Nature—Poetry. I. Homer, Winslow, 1836-1910.
II. Sargent, John Singer, 1856-1925. III. Sky-Peck,
Kathryn. IV. Museum of Fine Arts, Boston. V. Title.
VI. Title: Poet's Delay
PS3041.S58 1992   92-350
811'.3—DC20   CIP

ISBN 0-87846-354-2 (MFA)
ISBN 0-8478-1632-X (Rizzoli)

Design by Christopher Frame

...TED AND BOUND IN CHINA

CONTENTS

ACKNOWLEDGMENTS

We wish to acknowledge the first compilation of Thoreau's poetry, edited by Carl Bode and published in 1943. For many years it was the standard resource for these little known works. More recently, acknowledgments are due to Elizabeth Wethergell, Editor of Princeton University Press's undertaking of the publication of Thoreau's complete works. Ms. Wethergell's specialization in Thoreau's poetry proved invaluable. In this edition, further editorial refinements were made to some works based on the many versions of poems that Thoreau had scribbled throughout his journals. This was a fragile undertaking: to edit poems often not meant for publication, and in some cases, poems that were meant to be part of Thoreau's prose, or poems in which pages were torn or had pages missing from the original journals. We offer this not as a scholarly treatise, but to provide the reader easy access to the vision of Thoreau.

This project would not have been possible without access to Henry Thoreau's journals at the Thoreau Lyceum, Concord, Massachusetts. We would especially like to thank Dick O'Connor of the Thoreau Lyceum for his help on this project, and Thomas Blanding for his valuable insights into the life and work of Thoreau.

Special thanks are due to Sue Reed of the Prints and Drawing Department of the Museum of Fine Arts, Boston, and Eleanor Cappa, who helped make this publication possible.

INTRODUCTION

This is a book about nature, our world, and how we relate to it. It is meant to be a visual and auditory treat for the senses for all who love nature, art, and the music of language. When we considered such a project, it seemed only natural that we should turn to Henry Thoreau for that music, for not only is he known for his beautiful, lyrical and poetic prose, but he has also become somewhat of an icon of our age: the man who has become synonomous with nature, conservation and human morality.

Henry Thoreau is probably best known for his work *Walden*, but for years prior to its publication, Thoreau was busy at work as a poet, and speaks of himself in his early journals as a poet. One must understand "poet" in the true sense that the word held in the 19th century—Thoreau considered himself not a maker of poetic verses, but a man of poetic mind. A naturalist by heart and a perfectionist by nature, Thoreau used his poetry to exercise his craft as an essayist. His writing has been described as having "the vividness of a painter, and the scrutiny of a naturalist." Emerson exclaimed that Thoreau's poetry was "the purest and loftiest to sound" in the then "unpoetic American forest." For his subject matter Thoreau chose what mattered most to his life: unity. How does one live in nature and society, and lead a moral life?

As part of the transcendentalist movement of the 19th century, Thoreau believed strongly in the theory of transcendental inspiration and had high respect for the force of the "first thought." In a way, this accounts for his lack of notoriety as a poet—his legacy, after all, has come down to us through *Walden* and his essays. But it also gives us a special insight into his personal ethic: Thoreau's poems are snapshots of the world, succinctly, quickly and thriftily crafted. In this way, he is very much akin to the watercolorist who makes a striking and sweeping draft of a landscape, only to bring it home and build from it the larger, more detailed painting.

In this special book, Thoreau's poetry, rarely published, provides us with a detailed lens through which we can view his world—moments caught in amber. We've illustrated this work with watercolors by artists who share his ethic, and who were captivated by the nuances and fleeting delicacies of life. In this way, these, too, are portraits of a world seen through that same lens.

There are many misconceptions about Thoreau: that he was a hermit, lived in a tiny cabin in the woods, and lived off nuts and berries. In fact, Henry Thoreau was a very social man, a dedicated man, and an ethical man. He believed strongly in community, society, and how best humankind could live a moral life. Thoreau has come to represent for us the epitome of living in balance with nature, for without nature, without preserving the land, he knew that humanity would cease to exist.

But it's important to understand that Henry Thoreau was very much a part of society. Many people in the 1970's and early 80's dropped out of society in order to get "back to the land." But Henry Thoreau would have argued that society was a integral part of nature's harmony, and that we must act from within for change.

This book is dedicated to the Thoreau Country Conservation Alliance, and the Walden Woods Project, who are committed to preserving the wilderness as Thoreau knew it. This book is also dedicated to all conservation societies who have given their efforts to protecting our natural resources, and thus our planet and our existance.

And this book is dedicated to the most silent and threatened of our resources: our cultural resources. It is dedicated to the museums all over the country that house over 5,000 years of our human creative history.

We hope this book builds a bridge between the two: our precious natural and creative worlds. In Thoreau's own words:

"I have seen how the foundations of the world are laid, and I have not the least doubt that it will stand a good while. . . .

"If we will admit time into our thoughts at all, the mythologies, those vestiges of ancient poems, wrecks of poems, so to speak, the world's inheritance, still reflecting some of their original splendor, like the fragments of clouds tinted by the rays of the departed sun; reaching into the latest summer day, and allying this hour to the morning of creation . . . these are the materials and hints for a history of the rise and progress of the race; how, from the condition of ants, it arrived at the condition of men, and arts were gradually invented. Let a thousand surmises shed some light on this story."

Kathryn Sky-Peck
Museum of Fine Arts, Boston

My life has been the poem I would have writ,
But I could not both live and utter it.
　　　　　　　—HENRY DAVID THOREAU

HENRY DAVID THOREAU
THE POET'S DELAY

George Hallowell, *Trees in Winter*

WITHIN THE CIRCUIT OF THIS PLODDING LIFE

Within the circuit of this plodding life
There enter moments of an azure hue,
Untarnished fair as is the violet
Or anemone, when the spring strews them
By some meandering rivulet, which make
The best philosophy untrue that aims
But to console man for his grievances.

I have remembered when the winter came,
High in my chamber in the frosty nights,
When in the still light of the cheerful moon,
On every twig and rail and jutting spout,
The icy spears were adding to their length
Against the arrows of the coming sun;
How in the shimmering noon of summer past
Some unrecorded beam slanted across
The upland pastures where the Johnswort grew;
Or heard, amid the verdure of my mind,
The bee's long smothered hum, on the blue flag
Loitering amidst the mead; or busy rill,
Which now through all its course stands still and dumb
Its own memorial,—purling at its play
Along the slopes, and through the meadows next,
Until its youthful sound was hushed at last
In the staid current of the lowland stream;
Or seen the furrows shine but late upturned,
And where the fieldfare followed in the rear,
When all the fields around lay bound and hoar
Beneath a thick integument of snow.
So by God's cheap economy made rich
To go upon my winter's task again.

NATURE

O nature I do not aspire
To be the highest in thy choir,
To be a meteor in the sky
Or comet that may range on high—

Only a zephyr that may blow
Among the reeds by the river low.
Give me thy most privy place
Where to run my airy race.

In some withdrawn unpublic mead
Let me sigh upon a reed,
Or in the woods with leafy din
Whisper the still evening in.

For I had rather be a child
And pupil in the forest wild
Than be the king of men elsewhere
And most sovereign slave of care,

To have one moment of thy dawn
Than share the city's year forlorn.
Some humble work give me to do
If only it be near to you.

Winslow Homer, *Hudson River (Adirondacks)*, 1892

A WINTER AND SPRING SCENE

The willows droop,
The alders stoop,
The pheasants group
  Beneath the snow;

The fishes glide
From side to side,
In the clear tide,
  The ice below.

The ferret weeps,
The marmot sleeps,
The owlet keeps
  In his snug nook.

The rabbit leaps,
The mouse out-creeps,
The flag out-peeps,
  Beside the brook.

The snow-dust falls,
The otter crawls,
The partridge calls
  Far in the wood;

The traveller dreams,
The tree-ice gleams,
The blue jay screams
  In angry mood.

The apples thaw,
The ravens caw,
The squirrels gnaw
  The frozen fruit;

Frederick Childe Hassam, *Blossoming Trees*, 1882

Charles Emile Heil, *Road in Winter*

To their retreat
I track the feet
Of mice that eat
    The apple's root.

The axe resounds,
And bay of hounds,
And tinkling sounds
    Of wintry fame;

The hunter's horn
Awakes the dawn
On field forlorn,
    And frights the game.

The tinkling air
Doth echo bear
To rabbit's lair,
    With dreadful din;

She scents the air,
And far doth fare,
Returning where
    She did begin.

The fox stands still
Upon the hill
Not fearing ill
    From trackless wind.

But to his foes
The still wind shows
In treacherous snows
    His tracks behind.

Now melts the snow
In the warm sun.
The meadows flow,
    The streamlets run.

The spring is born,
The wild bees bum,
The insects hum,
    And trees drop gum.

And winter's gone,
And summer's come.

The chic-a-dee
Lisps in the tree,
The nuthatch creeps,
    the marmot sleeps;

George Hallowell, *Brook in Vermont*

The catkins green
Cast over the scene
A summer sheen,
    A genial glow.

I melt, I flow,
And rippling run,
Like melting snow
    In this warm sun.

THE STREAM

Some tumultuous little rill,
    Purling round its storied pebble,
Tinkling to the self-same tune,
From September until June,
    Which no drought doth ever enfeeble.

Silent flows the parent stream,
    And if rocks do lie below,
Smothers with her waves the din,
As if it were a youthful sin,
    Just as still, and just as slow.

TO A MARSH HAWK IN SPRING

There is health in thy gray wing
Health of nature's furnishing.
Say thou modern-winged antique,
Was thy mistress ever sick?
In each heaving of thy wing
Thou dost health and leisure bring,
Thou dost waive disease & pain
And resume new life again.

Frank Weston Benson, *Old Currituck Marshes, North Carolina*

UNTIL AT LENGTH THE NORTH WINDS BLOW

Until at length the north winds blow,
And beating high mid ice and snow,
        The sturdy goose brings up the rear,
Leaving behind the cold cold year.

Charles Burchfield, *In May*, 1939

MAY MORNING

The school boy loitered on his way to school,
Scorning to live so rare a day by rule.
So mild the air 'twas a pleasure to breathe,
For what seems heaven above was earth beneath.

Soured neighbors chatted by the garden pale,
Nor quarrelled who should drive the needed nail—
The most unsocial made new friends that day,
As when the sun shines husbandmen make hay.

How long I slept I know not, but at last
I felt my consciousness returning fast,
For Zephyr rustled past with leafy tread,
And heedlessly with one heel grazed my head.

My eyelids opened on a field of blue,
For close above a nodding violet grew,
A part of heaven it seemed, which one could scent,
Its blue commingling with the firmament.

I AM THE LITTLE IRISH BOY

I am the little Irish boy
      That lives in the shanty
I am four years old today
      And shall soon be one and twenty
      I shall grow up
      And be a great man
      And shovel all day
      As hard as I can

      Down in the deep cut
      Where the men lived
      Who made the rail road.

For supper
      I have some potatoe
      And sometimes some bread
      And then if it's cold
         I go right to bed.

      I lie on some straw
      Under my father's coat

      My mother does not cry
      And my father does not scold
      For I am a little Irish Boy
      And I'm four years old.

Jessie Wilcox Smith, *"When Daddy was a Little Boy,"* from *Rhymes of Real Children*, 1913

Henry Roderick Newman, *Hilly Landscape with Factories on a Riverbend*, 1867

THEY WHO PREPARE MY EVENING MEAL BELOW

They who prepare my evening meal below
Carelessly hit the kettle as they go
With tongs or shovel,
And ringing round and round,
Out of this hovel
It makes an eastern temple by the sound.

At first I thought a cow-bell right at hand
Mid birches sounded over the open land,
Where I plucked flowers
Many years ago,
Spending midsummer hours
With such secure delight they hardly seemed to flow.

TRAVELLING

How little curious is man—
He has not searched his mystery a span
But dreams of mines of treasure
Which he neglects to measure.

For three score years and ten
Walks to and fro amid his fellow men
Over this small tract of continental land
And never uses a divining wand.

Our uninquiring corpses lie more low,
Then our life's curiosity doth go
Our ambitious steps never climb so high
As in their hourly sport the sparrows fly.

And yonder cloud's borne farther in a day
Than our most vagrant feet may ever stray.
Surely, O Lord, he has not greatly erred,
Who has so little from his threshhold stirred.

He wanders through this low and shallow world
Scarcely his loftier thoughts and hopes unfurled,
Through this low walled world, where his huge sin
Has hardly room to rest and harbor in.

He wanders round until his end draws nigh
And then lays down his aged head to die—
And this is life, this is that famous strife.

Frederick Childe Hassam, *Canterbury*, 1889

Maurice Prendergast, *The Old West End Library, Boston (West Church)*, 1901

FOR THOUGH THE EAVES
WERE RABITTED

For though the eaves were rabitted,
     And the well sweeps were slanted,
Each house seemed not inhabited
     But haunted.

The pensive traveller held his way,
     Silent & melancholy,
For every man an idiot was,
     And every house a folly.

THE OLD MARLBOROUGH ROAD

Where they once dug for money,
But never found any;
Where sometimes Martial Miles
Singly files,
And Elija Wood,
I fear for no good:
No other man,
Save Elisha Dugan,—
O man of wild habits,
Partridges and rabbits,
Who has no cares,
Only to set snares,
Who lives all alone,
Close to the bone,
And where life is sweetest
Constantly eatest.
When the spring stirs my blood
With the instinct to travel,
I can get enough gravel
On the Old Marlborough Road.
Nobody repairs it,
For nobody wears it;
It is a living way,
As the Christians say.
Not many there be
Who enter therein,
Only the guests of the
Irishman Quin.
What is it, what is it,
But a direction out there,
And the bar possibility
Of going somewhere?
Great guide-boards of stone,
But travellers none;
Cenotaphs of the towns

Winslow Homer, *Woodsman and Fallen Tree (Adirondacks)*, (detail) 1891

Frank Weston Benson, *Old Tom*, 1923

Named on their crowns.
It is worth going to see
Where you might be.
What king
Did the thing,
I am still wondering;
Set up how or when,
By what selectman,
Gourgas or Lee,
Clark or Darby?
They're a great endeavor
To be something forever;
Blank tablets of stone,
Where a traveller might groan,
And in one sentence
Grave all that is known;
Which another might read,
In his extreme need.
I know one or two
Lines that would do,
Literature that might stand
All over the land,
Which a man could remember
Till next December,
And read again in the spring,
After the thawing.
If with fancy unfurled
You leave your abode,
You may go round the world
By the Old Marlborough Road.

LAST NIGHT AS I LAY GAZING

Last night as I lay gazing with shut eyes
                Into the golden land of dreams,
I thought I gazed down a quiet reach
           Of land and water prospect,
                Whose low beach
Was peopled with the now subsiding hum
Of happy industry—whose work is done.

And as I turned me on my pillow over,
I heard the lapse of waves upon the shore,
Distinct as it had been at broad noonday,
And I were wandering at Rockaway.

Winslow Homer, *Breaking Wave (Prout's Neck)*, 1887

James Wells Champney, *Artist in His Studio*, about 1880

INSPIRATION

I hear beyond the range of sound,
      I see beyond the range of sight,
New earths and skies and seas around,
      And in my noon the sun doth pale his light.

A clear and ancient harmony
      Pierces my soul through all its din,
As through its utmost melody—
      Further behind than they, further within.

More swift its bolt than lightning is,
      Its voice than thunder is more loud,
It expands my privacies
      To all, and leaves me single in the crowd.

It speaks with such authority,
      With so serene and lofty tone,
That idle Time runs gadding by,
      And leaves me with Eternity alone.

Always the general show of things
      Floats in review before my mind
And such true love and wonder brings
      That sometimes I forget that I am blind.

THE POET'S DELAY

In vain I see the morning rise,
    In vain observe the western blaze,
Who idly look to other skies,
    Expecting life by other ways.

Amidst such boundless wealth without,
    I only still am poor within,
The birds have sung their summer out,
    But still my spring does not begin.

Shall I then wait the autumn wind,
    Compelled to seek a milder day,
And leave no curious nest behind,
    No woods still echoing to my lay?

Winslow Homer, *The Adirondack Guide*, 1894

John Singer Sargent, *Carrara: Workmen*, 1911

CONSCIENCE IS INSTINCT BRED IN THE HOUSE

Conscience is instinct bred in the house,
Feeling and Thinking propagate the sin
By an unnatural breeding in and in.
I say, Turn it out doors,
Into the moors.
I love a life whose plot is simple,
And does not thicken with every pimple;
A soul so sound no sickly conscience binds it,
That makes the universe no worse than it finds it.

I love an earnest soul,
Whose mighty joy and sorrow
Are not drowned in a bowl,
And brought to life tomorrow;
That lives one tragedy,
And not seventy;
A conscience worth keeping,
Laughing not weeping;
A conscience wise and steady,
And forever ready;
Not changing with events,
Dealing in compliments;
A conscience exercised about
Large things, where one may doubt.

I love a soul not all of wood,
Predestinated to be good,
But true to the backbone
Unto itself alone,
And false to none;
Born to its own affairs,
Its own joys and own cares;
By whom the work which God begun
Is finished, and not undone;

Winslow Homer, *Tynemouth Sands*, 1882–1883

Taken up where he left off,
Whether to worship or to scoff;
If not good, why then evil,
If not good god, good devil.

Goodness! you hypocrite, come out of that,
Live your life, do your work, then take your hat.
I have no patience towards
Such conscientious cowards.
Give me simple laboring folk,
Who love their work,
Whose virtue is a song
To cheer God along.

CLIFFS

The loudest sound that burdens here the breeze
Is the wood's whisper; 'tis when we choose to list
Audible sound; and when we list not,
It is calm profound. Tongues were provided
But to vex the ear with superficial thoughts.
When deeper thoughts upswell, the jarring discord
Of harsh speech is hushed, and senses seem
As little as may be to share the extacy.

Charles William Hudson, *Spruce Tree in a Landscape*

Winslow Homer, *Driving Cows to Pasture*, 1879

WHAT'S THE RAILROAD TO ME?

What's the railroad to me?
I never go to see
Where it ends.
It fills a few hollows,
And makes banks for the swallows,
It sets the sand a-blowing,
And the blackberries a-growing.

OUR COUNTRY

It is a noble country where we dwell,
Fit for a stalwart race to summer in;
From Madawaska to Red River raft,
From Florid keys to the Missouri forks,
See what unwearied and copious streams
Come tumbling to the east and southern shore,
To find a man stand on their lowland banks:
Behold the innumerous rivers and the licks
Where he may drink to quench his summer's thirst,
And the broad corn and rice fields yonder, where
His hands may gather for his winter's store.

Frederick Childe Hassam, *The Knolls, N.H.*, 1917

Winslow Homer, *Palm Trees, Florida*, about 1904

See the fair reaches of the northern lakes
To cool his summer with their inland breeze,
And the long slumbering Appalachian range
Offering its slopes to his unwearied knees!
See what a long-lipped sea doth clip the shores,
And noble strands where navies may find port;
See Boston, Baltimore, and New York stand
Fair in the sunshine on the eastern sea,
And yonder too the fair green prairie.

See the native race with sullen step retreat,
Emptying its graves, striking the wigwam tent,
And where the rude camps of its brethren stand,
Dotting the distant green, their herds around;
In serried ranks, and with a distant clang,
Their fowl fly over, bound to the northern lakes,
Whose splashing waves invite their webbéd feet.

Such the fair reach and prospect of the land,
The journeying summer creeps from south to north
With wearied feet, resting in many a vale;
Its length tire the seasons to overcome,
Its widening breadth make the sea-breeze pause
And spend its breath against the mountain's side:
Still serene Summer paints the southern fields,
While the stern Winter reigns on northern hills.

Look nearer,—know the lineaments of each face,—
Learn the far-travelled race, and find here met
The so long gathering congress of the world!
The Afric race brought here to curse its fate,
Erin to bless,—the patient German too,
The industrious Swiss, the fickle, sanguine Gaul,
And manly Saxon, leading all the rest.
All things invite this earth's inhabitants

Thomas Moran, *Cliffs, Green River, Utah*, 1872

To rear their lives to an unheard-of height,
And meet the expectation of the land;
To give at length the restless race of man
A pause in the long westering caravan.

Andrew Wyeth, *Tilly Taggert*, 1948

INDEPENDENCE

My life is more civil and free
Than any civil polity.

Princes—keep your realms
And circumscribed power,
Not wide as are my dreams,
Nor rich as is this hour.

What can you give which I have not?
What can you take which I have got?
Can you defend the dangerless?
Can you inherit nakedness?

To all true wants time's ear is deaf,
Penurious states lend no relief
Out of their pelf—
But a free soul—thank God—
Can help itself.

Be sure your fate
Keeps apart its state—
Not linked with any band—
Even the nobles of the land

In tented fields with cloth of gold—
No place doth hold
But is more chivalrous than they are.
And sigheth for a nobler war.
A finer strain its trumpet rings—
A brighter gleam its armor flings.

The life that I aspire to live
No man proposeth me—
No trade upon the street
Wears its emblazonry.

THE RESPECTABLE FOLKS

The respectable folks—
Where dwell they?
They whisper in the oaks,
And they sigh in the hay
Summer and winter, night and day,
Out on the meadow, there dwell they.
They drink at the brooks and the pilgrim's cup,
And with the owl and the nighthawk sup;
They suck the breath of the morning wind,
And they make their own all the good they find.
A sound estate forever they mend,
To every asker readily lend,
To the ocean wealth,
To the meadow health,
To Time his length,
To the rocks strength,
to the stars light,
to the weary night,
To the busy day,
To the idle play,
And so their good cheer never ends,
For all are their debtors, and all are their friends.

Maurice Prendergast, *Carnival, Franklin Park,* 1897

John La Farge, *Seacape*, about 1880

THE MOON NOW RISES TO HER ABSOLUTE RULE

The moon now rises to her absolute rule,
And the husbandman and hunter
Acknowledge her for their mistress.
Asters and golden reign in the fields
And the life everlasting withers not.
The fields are reaped and shorn of their pride
But an inward verdure still crowns them
The thistle scatters its down on the pool
And yellow leaves clothe the river—
And nothing disturbs the serious life of men.
But behind the sheaves and under the sod
There lurks a ripe fruit which the reapers have not gathered
The true harvest of the year—the boreal fruit
Which it bears forever.
With fondness annually watering and maturing it.
But man never severs the stalk
Which bears this palatable fruit.

SALMON BROOK

Salmon Brook,
Penichook,
Ye sweet waters of my brain,
When shall I look,
Or cast the hook,
In your waves again?

Silver eels,
Wooden creels,
These the baits that still allure,
And dragon-fly
That floated by,
May they still endure?

Winslow Homer, *Ouananiche Fishing: Lake St. John, Province of Quebec,* 1897

Winslow Homer, *Leaping Trout (Adirondacks)*, 1892

VOYAGER'S SONG

Gentle river, gentle river
Swift as glides thy stream along,
Many a bold Canadian voyageur,
Bravely swelled the gay chanson

Thus of old our valiant fathers,
Many a lagging year agone
Gliding over the rippling waters,
Taught to banish care in song.

Now the sun's behind the willows,
Now he gleams along the lake,
Hark across the bounding billows
Liquid songs the echoes wake.

Rise Apollo up before us,
Even the lark's begun her lay
Let us all in deafening chorus
Praise the glorious king of day.

Thus we lead a life of pleasure,
Thus we while the hours away,
Thus we revel beyond measure,
Gaily live we while we may.

DELICATE FLOWER

I saw a delicate flower had grown up two feet high
Between the horse's paths and the wheel track
Which Dakin's and Maynard's wagons had
Passed over many a time—
An inch or more to right or left had sealed its fate
Or an inch higher. And yet it lived and flourished
As much as if it had a thousand acres
Of untrodden space around it—and never
Knew the danger it incurred.
It did not borrow trouble nor invite an
Evil fate by apprehending it.
For though the distant market-wagon
Every other day—inevitably rolled
In those ruts—And the same
Charioteer who steered the flower
Upward—guided the horse and cart aside from it.
There were other flowers which you would say
Incurred less danger grew more out of the way
Which no car rattled near, no walker daily passed.
But at length on rambling deviously,
For no rut restrained, plucked them
And then it appeared that they stood
Directly in his way though he had come
From farther than the market wagon—

Charles Demuth, *Zinnias and Daisies*, 1925

THE BLUEBIRDS

In the midst of the poplar that stands by our door,
We planted a bluebird box,
And we hoped before the summer was over
A transient pair to coax.

One warm summer's day the bluebirds came
And lighted on our tree,
But at first the wanderers were not so tame
But they were afraid of me.

They seemed to come from the distant south,
Just over the Walden wood,
And they skimmed it along with open mouth
Close by where the bellows stood.

Warbling they swept round the distant cliff,
And they warbled it over the lea,
And over the blacksmith's shop in a jiff
Did they come warbling to me.

They came and sat on the box's top
Without looking into the hole,
And only from this side to that did they hop,
As 'twere a common well-pole.

I had never seen them before,
Nor indeed had they seen me,
Till I chanced to stand by our back door,
And they came to the poplar tree.

In course of time they built their nest
And reared a happy brood,
And every morn they piped their best
As they flew away to the wood.

John James Audubon, *Blue-bird*, Plate CXIII

Thus wore the summer hours away
To the bluebirds and to me,
And every hour was a summer's day,
So pleasantly lived we.

They were a world within themselves,
And I a world in me,
Up in the tree—the little elves—
With their callow family.

One morn the wind blew cold and strong,
And the leaves went whirling away;
And the birds prepared for their journey long
That raw and gusty day.

Boreas came blustering down from the north,
And ruffled their azure smocks,
So they launched them forth, though somewhat loth,
By way of the old Cliff rocks.

Meanwhile the earth jogged steadily on
In her mantle of purest white,
And anon another spring was born
When winter was vanished quite.

And I wandered forth over the steamy earth,
And gazed at the mellow sky,
But never before from the hour of my birth
Had I wandered so thoughtfully.

For never before was the earth so still,
And never so mild was the sky,
The river, the fields, the wood, and the hill,
Seemed to heave an audible sigh.

I felt that the heavens were all around,
And the earth was all below,

As when in the ears there rushes a sound
Which thrills you from top to toe.

I dreamed that I was an awaking thought—
A something I hardly knew—
Not a solid piece, nor an empty nought,
But a drop of morning dew.

It was the world and I at a game of bo-peep,
As a man would dodge his shadow,
An idea becalmed in eternity's deep—
Between Lima and Segraddo.

Anon a faintly warbled note
From out of the azure deep
Into my ears did gently float
As like the approach of sleep.

It thrilled but startled not my soul;
Across my mind strange memories gleamed,
As often distant scenes unroll
When we have lately dreamed.

The bluebird had come from the distant south
To his box in the poplar tree,
And he opened wide his slender mouth,
On purpose to sing to me.

James Hamilton, *New Jersey Marshes*, (detail) 1861

I AM THE AUTUMNAL SUN

I am the autumnal sun,
With autumn gales my race is run;
When will the hazel put forth its flowers,
Or the grape ripen under my bowers?
When will the harvest or the hunter's moon,
Turn my midnight into mid-noon?
     I am all sere and yellow,
      And to my core mellow.
The mast is dropping within my woods,
The winter is lurking within my moods,
And the rustling of the withered leaf
Is the constant music of my grief.

WHERE GLEAMING FIELDS OF HAZE

Where gleaming fields of haze
Meet the voyageur's gaze,
And above, the heated air
Seems to make a river there,
The pines stand up with pride
By the Souhegan's side,
And the hemlock and the larch
With their triumphal arch
Are waving over its march
   To the sea.

Winslow Homer, *Adirondack Lake (Upper Ausable Lake)*, 1889

No wind stirs its waves,
But the spirits of the braves
        Hovering over,
Whose antiquated graves
Its still water laves
        On the shore.
With an Indian's stealthy tread,
It goes sleeping in its bed
Without joy or grief,
Or the rustle of a leaf,
Without a ripple or a billow,
Or the sigh of a willow,
From the Lyndeboro' hills
To the Merrimack mills.
With a louder din
Did its current begin,
When melted the snow
On the far mountain's bow,
And the drops came together
In that rainy weather.
Experienced river,
Have you flowed forever?
Souhegan sounds old,
But the half is not told,
What names have you borne,
In the ages far gone,
When the Xanthus and Meander
Commenced to wander,
Ere the black bear haunted
        Thy red forest-floor,
Or Nature had planted
        The pines by thy shore?

MEN SAY THEY KNOW MANY THINGS

Men say they know many things;
But lo! they have taken wings,—
The arts and sciences,
And a thousand appliances;

The wind that blows
Is all that any body knows.

EPITAPH ON THE WORLD

Here lies the body of this world,
Whose soul alas to hell is hurled.
This golden youth long since was past,
Its silver manhood went as fast,
And iron age drew on at last;
'Tis vain its character to tell,
The several fates which it befell,
What year it died, when it will arise—
We only know that here it lies.

Winslow Homer, *The Fallen Deer (Adirondacks)*, 1892

John La Farge, *Mountain Gorge near Dambulla, Ceylon*, 1891

FOG

Low-anchored cloud,
Newfoundland air,
Fountain-head and source of rivers,
Dew-cloth, dream drapery,
And napkin spread by fays;
Drifting meadow of the air,
Where bloom the daisied banks and violets,
And in whose fenny labyrinth
The bittern booms and heron wades;
Spirit of lakes and seas and rivers,
Bear only perfumes and the scent
Of healing herbs to just men's fields!

I AM BOUND FOR A DISTANT SHORE

I am bound, I am bound, for a distant shore,
By a lonely isle, by a far Azore,
There it is, there it is, the treasure I seek,
On the barren sands of a desolate creek.

MAN'S LITTLE ACTS ARE GRAND

Man's little acts are grand,
Beheld from land to land,
There as they lie in time,
Within their native clime.
      Ships with the noontide weigh,
      And glide before its ray
      To some retired bay,
      Their haunt,
      Whence, under tropic sun,
      Again they run
      Bearing gum Senegal and Tragicant.
For this was ocean meant,
For this the sun was sent,
And moon was lent,
And winds in distant caverns pent.

Winslow Homer, *The Sponge Diver (Bahamas)*, 1889

Winslow Homer, *Bridlington Quay, Yorkshire, England*, 1883

LOVE

We two that planets erst had been
Are now a double star,
And in the heavens may be seen,
Where that we fixed are.

Yet whirled with subtle power along,
Into new space we enter,
And evermore with spheral song
Revolve about one center.

THE ELM TREE

Upon the lofty elm tree sprays
The vireo rings the changes sweet,
During the trivial summer days,
Striving to lift our thoughts above the street.

CONSIGNED TO THE MUSES

I to nature consign.
I am but the word of myself.
Without inlet it lies,
Without outlet it flows . . .
From and to the skies
It comes and it goes . . .
I am its source,
And my life is its course;
I am its stoney shore
And the gale that passes over . . .

Henry Roderick Newman, *The Elm*, 1866

Frederick Childe Hassam, *Nocturne, Railway Crossing, Chicago*, early 1890s

I'M GUIDED IN THE DARKEST NIGHT

I'm guided in the darkest night
By flashes of auroral light,
Which over dart thy eastern home
And teach me not in vain to roam.
Thy steady light on the other side
Pales the sunset, makes day abide,
And after sunrise stays the dawn,
Forerunner of a brighter morn.

There is no being here to me
But staying here to be;
When others laugh I am not glad,
When others cry I am not sad;
But be they grieved or be they merry
I'm supernumerary.
I am a miser without blame
Am conscience stricken without shame.
An idler am I without leisure,
A busy body without pleasure.

I did not think so bright a day
Would issue in so dark a night.
I did not think such sober play
Would leave me in so sad a plight,
And I should be most sorely spent
Where first I was most innocent.
I thought by loving all beside
To prove to you my love was wide,
And by the rites I soared above
To show you my peculiar love.

CANS'T THOU LOVE WITH THY MIND?

Cans't thou love with thy mind,
    And reason with thy heart?
Cans't thou be kind,
    And from thy darling part?

Cans't thou range earth, sea, & air,
And so to meet me everywhere?
Through all events I will pursue thee,
Through all persons I will woo thee.

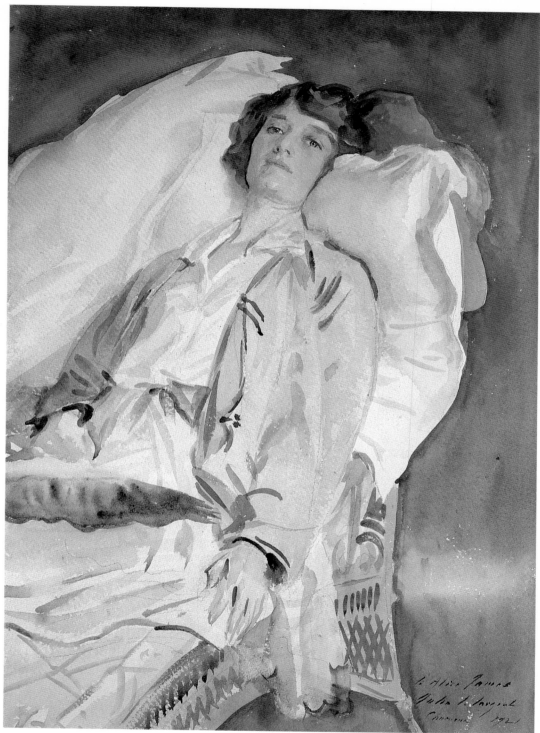

John Singer Sargent, *Portrait of Alice Runnells James*, 1921

John Singer Sargent, *Ladies Reading*, 1911

FRIENDS

Friends—
They cannot help,
They cannot hurt,
Nor indifference rest,
But when for a host's service girt,
They are a mutual guest.

They are a single power
Plenipotentiary,
No minister of state,
Anxious and wary
Decides their fate.

Where interest's self is
There is no go-between,
But where another reaps,
They do but glean
In scanty heaps.

They have learned well to hate,
And never grant reprieve,
Nor ever succumb to love,
But sternly grieve,
And look above.

If faults arise, my friend will send for me
As some great god,
Who will the matter try,
Holding the scales, even or odd,
Under the sky—

Who will award strict justice
All the while,
Confounding mine and thine,
And share his smile,
When they against me incline.

I DO NOT FEAR MY THOUGHTS WILL DIE

I do not fear my thoughts will die
For never yet it was so dry
As to scorch the azure of the sky.
It knows no withering & no drought
Though all eyes crop it never gives out
My eyes my flocks are
Mountains my crops are
I do not fear my flocks will stray
For they were made to roam the day
For they can wander with the latest light
Yet be at home at night.

Henry Loring Brown, *The Mythens Near Schwyz*, 1858

Winslow Homer, *Old Settlers (Adirondacks)*, about 1892

I WAS MADE ERECT AND LONE

I was made erect and lone
And within me is the bone
Still my vision will be clear
Still my life will not be drear
To the center all is near
Where I sit there is my throne
If age choose to sit apart
If age choose give me the start
Take the sap and leave the heart

THE INWARD MORNING

Packed in my mind lie all the clothes
        Which outward nature wears,
An in its fashion's hourly change
        It all things else repairs.

In vain I look for change abroad,
        And can no difference find,
Till some new ray of peace uncalled
        Illumes my inmost mind.

What is it gilds the trees and clouds,
        And paints the heavens so gay,
But yonder fast-abiding light
        With its unchanging ray?

Lo, when the sun streams through the wood,
        Upon a winter's morn,
Wherever his silent beams intrude
        The murky night is gone.

How could the patient pine have known
        The morning breeze would come,
Or humble flowers anticipate
        The insect's noonday hum,—

Till the new light with morning cheer
        From far streamed through the aisles,
And nimbly told the forest trees
        For many stretching miles?

I've heard within my inmost soul
        Such cheerful morning news,
In the horizon of my mind
        Have seen such orient hues,

John Singer Sargent, *Simplon Pass: Mountain Brook*, 1911

As in the twilight of the dawn,
    When the first birds awake,
Are heard within some silent wood,
    Where they the small twigs break,

Or in the eastern skies are seen,
    Before the sun appears,
The harbingers of summer heats
    Which from afar he bears.

James Fitzgerald, *Home by Moonlight*, about 1940

THE MOON

Time wears her not; she doth his chariot guide;
Mortality below here orb is placed.

—RALEIGH.

The full-orbed moon with unchanged ray
    Mounts up the eastern sky,
Not doomed to these short nights for aye,
    But shining steadily.

She does not wane, but my fortune,
    Which her rays do not bless,
My wayward path declineth soon,
    But she shines not the less.

And if she faintly glimmers here,
    And paled is her light,
Yet alway in her proper sphere
    She's mistress of the night.

RUMORS FROM AN AEOLIAN HARP

There is a vale which none hath seen,
Where foot of man has never been,
Such as here lives with toil and strife,
An anxious and a sinful life.

There every virtue has its birth,
Ere it descends upon the earth,
And there every deed returns,
Which in the generous bosom burns.

There love is warm, and youth is young,
And poetry is yet unsung,
For Virtue still adventures there,
and freely breathes her native air.

And ever, if you hearken well,
You still may hear its vesper bell,
And tread of high-souled men go by,
Their thoughts conversing with the sky.

John Singer Sargent, *Daphne*, about 1910

Charles Burchfield, *Winter Bouquet*, 1933

THOU DUSKY SPIRIT OF THE WOOD

Thou dusky spirit of the wood,
Bird of an ancient brood,
Flitting thy lonely way,
A meteor in the sumer's day,
From wood to wood, from hill to hill,
Low over forest, field and rill,
What wouldst thou say?
Why shouldst thou haunt the day?
What makes thy melancholy float?
What bravery inspires thy throat,
And bear thee up above the clouds,
Over desponding human crowds,
Which far below
Lay thy haunts low?

THE FALL OF THE LEAF

The evening of the year draws on,
      The fields a later aspect wear;
Since Summer's garishness is gone,
      Some grains of night tincture the noontide air.

Behold! the shadows of the trees
      Now circle wider about their stem,
Like sentries that by slow degrees
      Perform their rounds, gently protecting them.

And as the year doth decline,
      The sun allows a scantier light;
Behind each needle of the pine
      There lurks a small auxiliar to the night.

I hear the cricket's slumbrous lay
      Around, beneath me, and on high;
It rocks the night, it soothes the day,
      And everywhere is Nature's lullaby.

But most he chirps beneath the sod,
      When he has made his winter bed;
His creak grown fainter but more broad,
      A film of autumn over the summer spread.

Small birds, in fleets migrating by,
      Now beat across some meadow's bay,
And as they tack and veer on high,
      With faint and hurried click beguile the way.

Far in the woods, these golden days,
      Some leaf obeys its Maker's call;
And through their hollow aisles it plays
      With delicate touch the prelude of the Fall.

Frederick Childe Hassam, *Woods in the Fall*

John Singer Sargent, *The Shadowed Stream*

Gently withdrawing from its stem,
      It lightly lays itself along
Where the same hand had pillowed them,
      Resigned to sleep upon the old year's throng.

The loneliest birch is brown and sere,
      The furthest pool is strewn with leaves,
Which float upon their watery bier,
      Where is no eye that sees, no heart that grieves.

The jay screams through the chestnut wood;
      The crisped and yellow leaves around
Are hue and texture of my mood—
      And these rough burrs my heirlooms on the ground.

The threadbare trees, so poor and thin—
      They are no wealthier than I;
But with as brave a core within
      They rear their boughs to the October sky.

Poor knights they are which bravely wait
      The charge of Winter's cavalry,
Keeping a simple Roman state,
      Discumbered of their Persian luxury.

SMOKE

Light-winged smoke, Icarian bird,
Melting your wings in your upward flight,
Lark without song, and messenger of dawn,
Circling above the hamlets as your nest;

Or else, departing dream, and shadowy form
Of midnight vision, gathering up your skirts;
By night star-veiling, and by day
Darkening the light and blotting out the sun;

Go thou my incense upward from this hearth,
And ask the Gods to pardon this clear flame.

John La Farge, *Study for Spring*

George Hallowell, *Snow Drapery*

WHEN WINTER FRINGES EVERY BOUGH

When Winter fringes every bough
    With his fantastic wreath,
And puts the seal of silence now
    Upon the leaves beneath;

When every stream in its pent-house
    Goes gurgling on its way,
And in his gallery the mouse
    Nibbles the meadow hay;

I think the summer still is nigh,
    And lurketh underneath,
As that same meadow mouse doth lie
    Snug in the last year's heath.

And if perchance the chicadee
    Lisp a faint note anon,
The snow in summer's canopy,
    Which she herself put on.

Fair blossoms deck the cheerful trees,
    And dazzling fruits depend,
The north wind sighs a summer breeze,
    The nipping frosts to fend,

Bringing glad tidings unto me,
    The while I stand all ear,
Of a serene eternity,
    Which need not winter fear.

Out on the silent pond straightway
    The restless ice doth crack,
And pond sprites merry gambols play
    Amid the deafening rack.

Eager I hasten to the vale,
      As if I heard brave news,
How nature held high festival,
      Which it were hard to lose.

I gambol with my neighbor ice,
      And sympathizing quake,
As each new crack darts in a trice
      Across the gladsome lake.

One with the cricket in the ground,
      And faggot on the hearth,
Resounds the rare domestic sound
      Along the forest path.

Charles Emile Heil, *Snow Scene*, 1916

James Wells Champney, *Artist Sketching in a Park,* (detail)

IT IS NO DREAM OF MINE

It is no dream of mine,
To ornament a line;
I cannot come nearer to God and Heaven
Than I live to Walden even.
I am its stony shore,
And the breeze that passes over;
In the hollow of my hand
Are its water and its sand,
And its deepest resort
Lies high in my thought.

WHEN IN SOME COVE I LIE

When in some cove I lie,
A placid lake at rest,
Scanning the distant hills,
A murmur from the west,
And gleam of thousand rills
Which gently swell my breast,
Announce the friendly thought,
And in one wave sun-lit
I'm softly brought
Seaward with it.

I SAILED UP A RIVER

I sailed up a river with a pleasant wind,
New lands, new people, and new thoughts to find;
Many fair reaches and headlands appeared,
And many dangers were there to be feared;
But when I remember where I have been,
And the fair landscapes that I have seen,
THOU seemed the only permanent shore,
The cape never rounded, nor wandered over.

Winslow Homer, *Afterglow (Tynemouth, England)*, 1883

Winslow Homer, *The Blue Boat (Adirondacks)*, 1892

WALDEN

——True, our converse a stranger is to speech,
Only the practised ear can catch the surging words,
That break and die upon thy pebbled lips.
Thy flow of thought is noiseless as the lapse of thy own waters,
Wafted as is the morning mist up from thy surface,
So that the passive Soul doth breathe it in,
And is infected with the truth thou would express.

Even the remotest stars have come in troops
And stopped low to catch the benediction
Of thy countenance. Often as the day came round,
Impartial has the sun exhibited himself
Before thy narrow skylight—nor has the moon
For cycles failed to roll this way
As often as elsewhere, and tell thee of the night.
No cloud so rare but here it stalked,
And in thy face looked doubly beautiful.

O! tell me what the winds have written within these thousand years,
On the blue vault that spans thy flood—
Or the sun transferred and delicately reprinted
For thy own private reading. Somewhat
Within these latter days I've read,
But surely there was much that would have thrilled the Soul,
Which human eye saw not.

I would give much to read that first bright page,
Wet from a virgin press, when Eurus—Boreas—
And the host of airy quill-drivers
First dipped their pens in mist.

INDEX OF FIRST LINES

**John James Audubon
(American, 1785-1851)**
Blue-bird (Plate CXIII)
Etching and aquatint with handcoloring
by Robert Havell, Jr.
19¼ x 12⅜ inches
Gift of William Hooper
21.11772.113

**Frank Weston Benson
(American, 1862-1951)**
Old Currituck Marshes, North Carolina
Watercolor, 19¼ x 26⅜ inches
Gift of Mrs. Edward C. Storrow in
memory of her husband
33.589

Old Tom, 1923
Watercolor, 20¹/₁₆ x 14¹/₁₆ inches
Bequest of Mrs. Edward Jackson Holmes;
Edward Jackson Holmes Collection.
64.2104

**George Loring Brown
(American, 1814-1889)**
The Mythens Near Schwyz, 1858
Watercolor, 10⅜ x 17¹/₁₆ inches
Gift of Maxim Karolik   61.263

**Charles Burchfield
(American, 1893-1967)**
In May, 1939
Watercolor, 24½ x 19½ inches
Charles Henry Hayden Fund   39.762

Winter Bouquet, 1933
Watercolor and gouache over graphite,
35⅜ x 16¾ inches
Ellen Gardner Fund   34.43

**James Wells Champney
(American, 1845-1903)**
Artist Sketching in a Park
Watercolor on blue-gray paper,
5 x 9 inches
M. and M. Karolik Collection
58.1082

James Wells Champney
(American, 1845–1903)
Artist in His Studio, about 1880
Watercolor, 10⅝ x 14¼ inches
M. and M. Karolik Collection
58.1083

Charles Demuth
(American, 1883–1935)
Zinnias and Daisies, 1925
Watercolor, 17½ x 11⅝ inches
Frederick Brown Fund.
40.231

James Fitzgerald
(American, 1899–1971)
Home by Moonlight, about 1940
Watercolor, 18¾ x 25 inches
Gift of Mr. and Mrs. Edgar Hubert
1982.268

George Hallowell
(American, 1871–1926)
Brook in Vermont
Watercolor, 9¾ x 13½ inches
Ross Collection. Gift of Denman W. Ross.
06.122

Trees in Winter
Watercolor, 20 x 14½ inches
Gift of Frederick L. Jack
35.1234

Snow Drapery
Watercolor, 20 x 14-1/2 inches
Gift of Frederick L. Jack
35.1233

James Hamilton
(American, 1819–1878)
New Jersey Marshes, 1861
Watercolor, 8-7/8 x 16-5/8 inches
Gift of Maxim M. Karolik
61.283

Frederick Childe Hassam
(American, 1859–1935)
Blossoming Trees, 1882
Watercolor, 10½ x 9 inches
Bequest of Kathleen Rothe
65.1301

Canterbury, 1889
Watercolor on paper,
13½ x 9½ inches
Gift of the heirs of
Elizabeth A. Cotton
33.526

The Knolls, N.H., 1917
Watercolor over pencil,
10 x 14 inches
Bequest of Kathleen Rothe
65.1302

Nocturne, Railway Crossing, Chicago,
early 1890s
Watercolor, 15-1/2 x 11 inches
Charles Henry Hayden Fund
62.986

Woods in the Fall
Watercolor, 14 x 10 inches
Bequest of Kathleen Rothe
65.1300

**Charles Emile Heil
(American, 1870–1950)**
Road in Winter
Watercolor on paper
Bequest of John T. Spaulding
48.792

Snow Scene, 1916
Graphite & watercolor,
12⅛ x 11⅛ inches
Bequest of John T. Spaulding
48.797

**Winslow Homer
(American, 1836–1910)**
The Adirondack Guide, 1894
Watercolor on paper,
15 x 21½ inches
Bequest of Mrs. Alma H. Wadleigh
47.268

*Adirondack Lake
(Upper Ausable Lake),* 1889
Watercolor on paper, 14 x 20 inches
Warren Collection.
William Wilkins Warren Fund
23.215

*Afterglow
(Tynemouth, England),* 1883
Watercolor on paper,
15 x 21½ inches
Bequest of William P. Blake in memory
of his mother,
Mary M.J. Dehon Blake
22.606

The Blue Boat (Adirondacks), 1892
Watercolor on paper,
15⅛ x 21¼ inches
Bigelow Collection. Bequest of
William Sturgis Bigelow
26.764

Breaking Wave (Prout's Neck), 1887
Watercolor on paper,
15¼ x 21½ inches
Bigelow Collection. Bequest of
William Sturgis Bigelow
26.788

*Bridlington Quay,
Yorkshire, England,* 1883
Watercolor, 12½ x 15¼ inches
Bequest of Ralph W. Gray in memory
of his father, Samuel S. Gray
44.681

**Winslow Homer
(American, 1836–1910)**
Driving Cows to Pasture, 1879
Watercolor on paper,
8½ x 13⅝ inches
Bequest of the Estate of Katherine Dexter
McCormick
68.569

The Fallen Deer (Adirondacks), 1892
Watercolor on paper,
13¾ x 19¾ inches
Hayden Collection. Charles Henry
Hayden Fund
23.443

Hudson River (Adirondacks), 1892
Watercolor on paper, 14 x 20 inches
Bigelow Collection. Bequest of
William Sturgis Bigelow.
26.785

Leaping Trout (Adirondacks), 1892
Watercolor on paper, 14 x 20 inches
Warren Collection. William Wilkins
Warren Fund.
99.24

Old Settlers (Adirondacks),
about 1892
Watercolor on paper, 21 x 15 inches
Gift of Nathaniel T. Kidder
38.1412

*Ouananiche Fishing: Lake St. John,
Province of Quebec*, 1897
Watercolor on paper,
14 x 20¾ inches
Warren Collection. William Wilkins
Warren Fund.
99.30

Palm Trees, Florida, about 1904
Watercolor on paper,
19⅛ x 13½ inches
Bequest of John T. Spaulding
48.731

The Sponge Diver (Bahamas), 1889
Watercolor on paper,
13½ x 19 inches
Gift of Mrs. Robert B. Osgood
39.621

Tynemouth Sands, 1882–1883
Watercolor on paper,
13¾ x 20¼ inches
Gardner Brewer Collection.
Bequest of Mrs. Arthur Croft
01.6232

*Woodsman and Fallen Tree
(Adirondacks)*, 1891
Watercolor on paper, 14 x 20 inches
Bigelow Collection. Bequest of
William Sturgis Bigelow
26.778

**Charles William Hudson
(American, 1871–1943)**
Spruce Tree in a Landscape
Watercolor on paper, 30 x 22 inches
Gift of Miss Maria Hudson in memory
of the artist, her brother.
45.907

**John La Farge
(American, 1835–1910)**
*Mountain Gorge near Dambulla,
Ceylon,* 1891
Watercolor on paper,
17 x 13½ inches
Bigelow Collection. Bequest of
William Sturgis Bigelow   26.784

Seascape, about 1880
Watercolor, 6¹¹⁄₁₆ x 5 inches
Gift of Miss Mary C. Wheelwright
59.688

*Study for Window of "Spring"
for W. C. Whitney*
Watercolor on paper,
6¼ x 6¹⁄₁₆ inches
Bequest of John T. Spaulding
48.812

**Thomas Moran
(American, 1837–1926)**
Cliffs, Green River, Utah, 1872
Watercolor, 6³⁄₁₆ x 11¹¹⁄₁₆ inches
M. & M. Karolik Collection
60.428

**Henry Roderick Newman
(American, 1843–1917)**
The Elm, 1866
Watercolor, 16⅞ x 9⁵⁄₁₆ inches
M. and M. Karolik Collection
1973.380

*Hilly Landscape with Factories
on a Riverbed,* 1867
Watercolor, 10⁷⁄₁₆ x 13⅞ inches
Gift of Mrs. Harriet Ropes Cabot
50.2630

**Maurice Prendergast
(American, 1859–1924)**
Carnival, Franklin Park, 1897
Watercolor on paper,
13 x 14½ inches
Gift of the Estate of Nellie P. Carter
35.1689

*The Old West End Library, Boston
(West Church),* 1901
Watercolor on paper, 10⅞ x 15¾ inches
Hayden Collection.
Charles Henry Hayden Fund
58.1199

**John Singer Sargent
(American, 1856–1925)**
Carrara: Workmen, 1911
Watercolor on paper, 14 x 19¾ inches
Hayden Collection
Charles Henry Hayden Fund.
12.235

**John Singer Sargent
(American, 1856-1925)**
Daphne, about 1910
Watercolor on paper, 21 x 16 inches
Hayden Collection.
Charles Henry Hayden Fund.
12.230

Ladies Reading, 1911
Watercolor on paper, 20 x 14 inches
Hayden Collection.
Charles Henry Hayden Fund.
12.214

Portrait of Alice Runnells James, 1921
Watercolor on paper,
21⅛ x 13½ inches
Gift of William James
1977.834

The Shadowed Stream
Watercolor on paper,
13½ x 9½ inches
Zoë Oliver Sherman Collection.
Gift of Mrs. Henry H. Sherman.
23.727

Simplon Pass: Mountain Brook, 1911
Watercolor on paper, 14 x 20 inches
Hayden Collection.
Charles Henry Hayden Fund.
12.213

**Jessie Wilcox Smith
(American, 1863-1935)**
*"When Daddy was a Little Boy,"
from Rhymes of Real Children*
(New York, 1913)
Color relief, 8½ x 7¾ inches
Anonymous Gift

**Andrew Wyeth
(American, born 1917)**
Tilly Taggert, 1948
Watercolor, 23⅛ x 29¼ inches
Bequest of the Estate
of Katharine Dexter
67.986